The Cantor Set

(A Perfect Set that is Nowhere Dense*)

The Cantor Set

Julie Weber

Love's Body

Copyright © 2012. Julie Weber. All rights reserved.

Contents

Moth Wings Bare

Ides of March

Pontifical

Wolf Snow

Elytra

The Bruise

Myrrh

Swifts

The Relapsing Moon

Albedo

Tungsten

Reading Bones

Cornflower

Star Magnolia

Copper Underwing

Xanadu

Higher Math

The Eye of God

The Other that is Ourselves

Permutations

Afterword

Notes to the Poems

Moth Wings Bare

The smoke at Vespers, you tell me
(though we haven't talked in months)
isn't from an Oregon forest fire, no—

this hush that bears its ash
across the browbone of my birthday
comes from Russia. The smoke

that arced from Siberia to Alaska,
down through Canada, has settled now
into the Northwest.

Five hundred forests
are on fire, bones and whisper
of Baryshnikov's ancestors

reminding me of the way I once
too made an aerial leap
across my own Bering Strait

queer, bare and laid open
with all I was bearing,
your mouth covered

with all you weren't saying,
the hock of my heels falling,
unable, either of us, to complete

that sanctioned step—
the one where you catch
and lower me safely,

landing me—
mothwings full
of night's tender elasticity.

Now, instead, peat bogs burn,
and there is no saying
how many more months they could smolder,

if again they will flare,
or if again smoke will carry
the tendril of my extending ankle,

clarifying or clouding
your bare arm, stretched
and reaching across the Nome.

Tonight, in the Bel Air hills,
staring at a Sycamore
outside a 3rd story window,

I am wondering if, in our nocturne,
like moths, we angle our flight pattern
to the luminosity of celestial bodies,

or if instead we wear (as some scientists say)
Mach rings, dark wedding bands
that distort light and dark, loss and gift,

while we utter
the leaps and breaks
we are known by.

Ides of March

I know you think that was the day
of our undoing, your confession, veil lifting
on the coffers of quarantined information.

Once you began telling you couldn't stop.
You spent days unshanking leaves
from black poplars, Book of the Untold,
so busy your hands filling the air you couldn't see

long shadows already heaving
their gryphon wings, populating
the sky with apocryphal sound.

Your words pushed their long expulsion
with the pressure it had taken to contain them,
the inverse power with which you once
held your breath. It wasn't a Tango,

not even a conversation.
You could-not-see me,
the long plank of my body falling back
those weeks preceding your confession,

though I remember well
how I reached for you,
your moon pulled up short.

Now we both dwell in a concave
of bone and hush, sleeping with a collar
of ghost duff. I don't think of pity. I don't

think of blame. I simply notice, at night,
when I lay my head down
in the wheel well of the moon,

feathers and dry needles,
dust and stone. I set my cheek beneath
downed branch and twine, my camp

a high crux among switchblades,
a long path across a deteriorating bridge,
the beginning of that No Trespassing zone.

Pontifical

I haven't been to the secret meeting of you,
the pontificator's parlor of radioactivity

a vault that reminds me so much of the Vatican,
the way Michelangelo once stretched the hand of God
down

to touch a man, and then the Church
banished touch between them, chlorophyll

cut from calyx, leaving only
the dried tears of resinous trees,

sap squeezed of seizure,
sediment of longing. The touch

that was our palms
has become a books of psalms,

missiles sung only once
every 168 hours. Can you see

how close that is to religion? the way I was
stunned, shunned, cast out from the bylines —

You call that scripture?
I am unable to pray at that pew.

Wolf Snow

Sometimes I am not sure which of you
I love, the one who is a silhouette,

holding your power, or you. The irony
of the light version or the dark. His child, your child

said hello to me, his long hair falling
in a cascade of wolf snow, the old ice of it broken

by his eyes, cups of crystalline glass
turned to gather the world's water.

Sometimes I think if it were different,
I would be one to help with reentry,

my status a leverage, my psychology
a kind that can bridge Bering straits, the outskirts,

the exclave, the permafrost wetlands…
I don't want your oil — nor graupel —

your disguise, nor revelation. Stop acting
the miser. I haven't come for it. I am not coming.

I simply live down the street in this land called the Bush,
no roads, only the state's Forget Me Not flower.

Elytra

This is my crime, the way
I can't quite seem to close
my blue green sheath wings,
the elytra wanting only to open
the Electra of my thighs, still unmarked
like parchment craving a moving hand of ink,
the press of the curled palm's flute
finally warming a surface, marking it,
its heel to new skin.
When I am most in grief, I want only
the kind of submission that finds
warmth and safety. I fantasize again
about being homeless — the only time in life
touch has been within reach. I want to sleep
in the rattle of gravel under bridges
witnessed by the moon in train cars.
I want to undress
back to my life as Hobo,
the one in which we don't come home
to four walls, but curl our bodies and blankets together,
poverty and comfort like knuckles lacing gnarled hands,
the life where when I am alone,
it's common, and legitimized.

I carry a photograph by Nicole Blaisdell
that never leaves the small of my back.
If we were to unpack my backpack it would be
an epigraph from my collar of aspiration.

I want to dance/ in the field/ in my overalls
like that Bohemian couple, glass in hand
pressed to your back, eyes closing softly
as you lead a step of tenderness, no witness
but the cricket, the bullfrog, the loon.

I ripped Nicole's photo years ago

from pages of The Sun Magazine
and I have carried it like an expatriate carries
an image of her homeland, my own sphere
rolled with longing, spun
with the husk and hull of every love
that has fallen away,
ground to ash and filigree, leaf vein and decay,
wheeled together in a ball of scarab dung
rolling through a dark sleeve.

The Bruise

This is my masochism,
the way I can't quite close the valve
that is between us. You don't see it.
You can't seem to see that you are the valve
between me and something throwing a kink
in my RNA, the replicating code.

Behind you there is a complex
siphoning my marrow, damaging
white blood cells, altering my chemistry.

I hold you at bay because it breaks
the circuitry, my proximity to the damage,
the way damage spreads like a bruise
slow heaving even long after the point of impact,
the way healing lymph is clamped out
because the valve of you is a barrier.
You intend it and you don't,
this one way door, your shudder stop
perverting the power, your arms
reaching toward me, but your face
falling back to hear the undertaker.

By this formula
you and I are destined only ever to meet
in black poplars, the sound of hush, a wingspan.

Myrrh

The way the tree is cut
and bled: an incest that prospers, fallows
and consecrates its resin,
a sadness evocative
as sweetness on the day I found it

in a Satori Long Life Tea can,
tooled in the roots of a redwood,
beside the grate of Mason's tombs
beneath the Book of Padhmasambhava.
I opened the book: A Journey
in the Cemetery of Mysterious Apparitions
where he earned the name Todreng Tsal,
Strength of the Rosary of Skulls.

I am each bead, traded and sold,
strung and unstrung. Charcoal
blistering, the way a match rolls through,
a simmer of stars scintillating:
blooming and fading in quantum flush,
each red coal of heat aging with ash,
the black of pith worthy
of ecstasy and grief,
a caesura of saints,
tears watering bone.

Swifts

You don't float, or sway,
you puncture your hands
too close to my face,
like birds in the shape of swifts,
now a flock of them,
shoulders close to your ears.

Do you know you are
that much taller than me?
a chimneysweep
sky god of intensity,
hovering and puncturing
my atmosphere,
your wings
jambing my occult membrane.

Can you please
just learn
where I begin? My skin
is inimical
to this kind of siege.

The Relapsing Moon

Blue midnight, a cobalt cloud
   opaque and dense.
      We tried to swim through

the blown conspiracy of stars and planets,
   their disintegrating velvet backdrop
      wet and cloying, condensing

its mantle, a sinter
   on our shoulders,
      minerals and the gunmetal sky.

I tried to push
   my voluminous hands
      toward you, but my lungs

silted with slurry,
   the fine porcelain dust
      of old dolls.

Underwater,
   a wreckage of coral,
      the grey white scent of shatter

sharp
   exoskeletons
      cutting alveoli.

You were unable to find
   the pearl
      in my throat

your guilt: the relapsing moon,
    an albatross, a ruffle,
        your hair—like sea wrack.

I am not entirely sure
    how to feed us now,
        ghosts stammering the mineral scoured shore.

Albedo

Your window
is the port of a ship
octagonal,
and I am outside,
driving by,
watching the moon
tread water,
watching her reach
her hands
like foil
through its
envelope above you,
slipping her hair
though the peeled paint
and weathered pane.

I am outside
starboard, and underwater.
I am an octopus
with eight arms.
Not a single one
knows what to do.
I comb through sea kelp
and bladderwrack,
my whole body a muscle.

I lay myself out
a long way from the surface,
pull from my underarm
all my milkcreampearly moons,
hang them in strings
from the ceiling of my lairfall,

a bed of filament
hung with eggsac ornaments

the Star of Lakshmi
beneath a cathedral of bloom.

Tungsten

The soot
and the cream,
they mix on your coat
your guard hair
a crest
of halogen needles,
a mantle of Tungsten.

You are on
blades,
on sharps,
on electrodes
for pain.

You are brittle
and hard to find,

worthy of
an elemental label.

You are
the Moon's froth in 1747

the year Wallerius
discovered heavy stone,
a steel gray
forge and sinter.

You are ductile,
the weight of froth
in the white of wolfsbane.

Reading Bones

It's as uncomfortable for me as it is
for you. We don't meet eyes. We tuck
the froth of knowing under our armor.
It's not war, it's a grace called privacy,
you shoveling mulch, gravel,
me in the worn hock of tannin leaves
reading bones, the squall of radius and ulna
catching light on the ground like runes,
spelling — but not spelling — the heft
of that last thing they held.

Neither tuck of root nor stone
syndicate the telling. Far
from the scapulimancy of seers
the earth chelates the apatite of bone in the vertisol
until it is but a huck on the blanket of trail,
regolith of acorn and seedpod, usnea and snail shell
ground to the biomantle of everything
that shall go untold, the nestled branch,
the vine clad mountain laurel,
dried and hung with its handkerchiefs of lace,
the astragals of stardust too a shatter,
a slow grind of carbon to granite's armor.

Cornflower

If I were to pick up the phone,
if I were to call you or be able to call
on this day the sun has sideswiped
all the leaves of September, I'd lead you
by my cowbell of field horn
to a bridge that thumbs
roots of large leaf maples.

I'd hold open the sky and walk you
toward that slant of color.

I'd lay my calla hair,
ruddy with blown grass and oatfall,
down to the sun's bask of your tenured thigh,
the oracle of leaf and shadow,
the fierce net of leaves above
and the crisp curl of creek below,
holding and winnowing out,
carrying away the crosshatch,
mending even the way chicory is shaken,
its blue so like cornflowers, tiny dials,
the tenderest clock of time
kept by my eyelashes on your arm.

Copper Underwing

It's a natural riddle. *What Am I?*
We might as well be written in the Book of Exeter,
hovering like the Copper Underwing
I saw last night beneath the nest of black widows,

though its underwings
were not copper, but in full display
a warm dusty gray, with the mark
of the old world Mormo Maura,
a species unknown to the rustic Oregon biosphere.

I comb jpegs, guidebooks.

What am I? It's a natural riddle.

A sphinx
waiting to devour incarnations
that can't ken the city?
The homunculus of us,
a kenning, a secret glossary
of lingual nerves and tympani chords
a slip, a parapraxis?

You and I have always had
these interstices of communion,
the word play and neologism of dreams,

the sphinx waiting at the gate of waking,

spaces between when you call me
and when I let myself lay in your arms.

There is no where else
I ever rest.

I take the Copper Underwing to bed,

the Io moth and dusk of ferns,

the density of water
I carry in my breastplate,

the logarithm of longing

a math of muscles
that move and roll
from base to fractal,
the curvature of experience,
the carapace of desire.

Star Magnolia

I suffer blunt hands of the star magnolia
fisting out stout fingers, long enough
to reach the cedar of your hair, tear fistfuls
of needles to my skin, roll my stomach
with incense and indentation.

Strong enough to bear the sharpness
of the way your misunderstandings
have scraped and scratched their irritation,
a cloudbank of goodbyes
in the rib cage of each summer day,
my heart breaking a crush of atmosphere
to my body's rain. Even in the long dry
huff of the summer, your roots are drinking.

Xanadu

> *The mind paces in its beautiful error.*
> Stacie Cassarino

Capriole is a dance step an astrologer
once accused me of imagining, telling me I had invented

my *Lipizzans*, the interpretation
a sleight to trump the soul's ancestry,

defying hormones that stir a fetus to labor.
Ir Rahman, Ir Rahim... Once upon a time,

no one believed in an acrobatics of the equine line,
didn't recognize the Fibonacci code or the whorl

of hooves tracing the golden mean,
Cordoban sweat of my neck thick with doves,

pearlescent with rain, muscles plucking
the slow twitch sinews of a bass clef,

reconfiguring gravity. Now we have —
girls that are bois that write gay men's erotica

and psychotherapists that *fouette* a dance pole,
having never stopped feeding the bloodline of Pluto.

It's time to clean the Augean stables
where *Alph the sacred river ran ...*

Weave the circle round hym thrice...
hys flashing eyes, hys floating hair. Who

are we singling out and fixing
with the inimical eye? "Kubla Khan" says Charles Lamb,

"is an owl that won't bear daylight,"
a *strigiforme* not well subject to scrutiny,

yet I bring my creature from the sunless sea
mane and turret, hoof and heel pressed among mortals.

Higher Math

The missing third is consciousness
and my unwillingness to settle for less.

Said. Marked. A time lapse photograph
where the middle falls out in constant succession,

even when it is repeated, and magnified.
Your lives have cast you in armor.

I have no armor. Both your clumsiness
and obstinacy cause me harm. Physical harm.

Immunological harm. Psychological harm.
You can't hear me when I warn you

because you are not willing to postulate
my coordinates of sensitivity, giftedness, or damage.

I am not on your map. You are
rational numbers and I am composed

side by side, above and beyond,
by algebraics and transcendentals

you can't fathom exist. You dilate,
but add, subtract, multiply and divide

only your familiar integers
to staple your feet to the ground.

Mathematical laws fall into place
under our footsteps. The fallout between us

is a constant: a transfinite sequence,
and, but for our subjectivity, bears a strange beauty.

The Eye of God

Just as the ternary disappears with you,
so it is inside me, between me
and this inscrutable needle, the fabric
endlessly stitching on the loom.

So we hold the tiniest whorled sea shell.
I hear your voice in the cochlea of my ear.
The cusp of DNA expands and contracts,
spirals in and out, this
thyrsus pinecone and that galactic center,
the probability of density
whistling its song.

The Other, Ourselves

The scales of the dragon
are replicating fractals

upon that mystical creature
Draconis

where the only visible points
are *caput* and *cauda*,

each planet bouncing its nodes
through our incarnations

as we try to divine
the larger fractal of its form

the formulary of shape and meaning

through the transubstantiation
of points that cross our vector of vision.

The underpinning
of mathematical possibilities

is warp and weft
of our trajectories

as we try to grasp the soul

through the chart
of what it has reckoned with,

a body scaled in
in the fabric of lifetimes.

Permutations

I revisit you
the same way I revisit
the invisible hand stitching the loom.
I contemplate the intrinsic pattern
of lapses
upon the day, the month, the hour.

I see less of you — or more,
dilating — myself
in and out fractals
of the selfsame sequence,
making love to the very thing I love
in the absence
I can't understand,
in the presence of which
I am but a permutation,
and yet only in my participation —
this chance to grasp magnitude.

*   *   *   *   *

Afterword

When The Cantor Set came in a dream, I picked up a study of Georg Cantor and higher mathematics.

Georg Cantor (pronounced GAY-ork KAN-tur) revolutionized mathematics by identifying and proving we know less than we know. He was the first (known) mathematician to state that the world of real numbers, which includes transfinite numbers, is larger than our world of known numbers and fractions. We count natural numbers, but will never identify all the transcendental numbers, (even though we can identify some).

(There are basic notes on differences between real and natural numbers in the Notes section.)

Georg Cantor (1845-1918), born in St. Petersburg, was of Danish descent on his father's side and Hungarian Jewish descent on his mother's. Cantor has been called Danish, Russian, German, Jewish and Portuguese. His father initially had fled the Napoleonic wars in Copenhagen to St. Petersburg, and then the family moved to Germany when Georg was eleven.

Cantor revolutionized mathematics and philosophy akin to the way Copernicus revolutionized astronomy and Einstein physics.

His work was met with harsh opposition. His ideas were called "a grave disease." Cantor was viewed by many of his contemporaries as a "scientific charlatan," "renegade" and "corrupter of youth." One of the critiques of Cantor was that his Set theories and theories about transfinite numbers were blowing apart religion. Cantor countered this attesting that his work had spiritual coherence and that it not only had been communicated by the divine, but that it amplified our understanding of it.

Though Cantor spent the latter half of his life skillfully dismantling affronts to his theories, he was nonetheless discouraged by decades of derision. Georg was hospitalized twice for depression. Alternately, he took respite discussing implications of mathematics in Departments of Philosophy.

"The essence of Mathematics resides in its freedom," asserted Cantor, a statement that still bears reference to freedom from modes of thinking that perpetuate limited understanding and the tendency we have to self-project. Georg Cantor is best known and remembered today as the founder of Set theory.

Cantor Sets appear in a foreshortened form on the cover of this book of poems. The brackets above and below the image of Saturn show lines with one third of the line — the middle section — removed, becoming sets of lines where a middle section is again removed... This pattern has no end: it is transfinite (infinite), a fractal pattern that repeats without an ending number or decimal.

The Rings of Saturn are Cantor Sets.

Georg Cantor, "Uber Unedliche, Lineare Punktmanniischfaltigkeiten," *Mathematische Annalen*, 1883.

Biographical Information was collected from Wikipedia and online sources. Clifford Pickover has introductory segments on Georg Cantor in *A Passion for Mathematics: Numbers, Puzzles, Madness, Religion and the Quest for Reality* and in *The Loom of God: Tapestries of Mathematics and Mysticism*.

Notes:

Moth Wings Bare: is set against the backdrop of the Russian fires of August 2010.

Mach bands are a visual distortion where natural gradations between light and dark appear more pronounced when placed side by side. In the case of moths, this applies to artificial lights as well as to dark areas in the sky toward which the moths gravitate before entering the warp of the Mach band. Mach bands are said to circumscribe the earth's atmosphere, and in them, gradations of light create optical illusions.

Ides of March: Black Poplars line the entrance to the Underworld.

Pontifical: Incense used by the Catholic church is composed of frankincense, myrrh and resins bled from trees after they have been wounded.

Elytra: Nicole Blaisdell's photograph has been reproduced from The Sun Magazine to the cover of a book published by The Sun called *The Mysterious Life of the Heart*.

Myrrh: Myrrha had sex with her father, and, in the myths, when her father flew into a rage, the gods turned her into a tree. Her tears of grief for the way her love had been maligned became resins from the tree, used as incense. Adonis, a central figure in women's mystery traditions, was born from the union of Myrrha and her father. Myrrha is also the name of a kind of beetle.

The Relapsing Moon: *Scent of Shatter* is the name of a chapbook by Valerie Wetlaufer, printed by Grey Book Press. (Sinter is in the notes for Tungsten.)

Albedo: Octopus limbs are muscular hydrostats. They have no bones, three hearts and are highly intelligent. When an octopus is fertilized by another octopus's arm, she lays close to 200,000 eggs which hang in string-like formation in her nesting place in the sea.

Lakshmi is a goddess of fortune and fertility. The Sanskrit root *laks* means *to perceive or observe,* the concentrated and far reaching power of perception being connected with the bringing forth of luck and fertililty. The star of Lakshmi is an eight pointed star.

Tungsten: Tungsten is an elemental metal, also know as wolfram, translated literally as wolf soot, wolf froth or wolf cream. Sintering is a metallurgy term in which minerals are induced to adhere to each other. A sinter is a crust made from minerals by heat and/or pressure, without entirely melting the minerals. In geology, sinters are sometimes visible near springs where minerals have cooled and hardened at the earth's surface. Tungsten has the highest melting point of all non-alloyed metals and is worked by sintering, forging, drawing and extruding. Highly prized, very pure Tungsten is ductile, malleable, but the more commonly found Tungsten with minor impurities is brittle. The froth of wolframite is what dries or crusts into Tungsten. (Wolframite is found in quartz veins and granite intrusions).

Wolfsbane (monkshood or aconite) is a plant both medicine and poison.

Reading Bones: Scapulimancy is the oracular reading of bones. Apatite is the mineral component of teeth or bones and some mineral phosphates. Vertisol is the clay component of soil that shrinks or cracks and self mulches. Regolith is a blanket of dirt and dust that covers rock and exists on earth, on the moon and on some planets and asteroids. Astragals are knuckle bones, or ankle bones, used in games and divination. They refer to the beading of stars and crossings of fate.

Cornflower: The cowbell is sacred to Hathor, a goddess of Ancient Egypt.

Gates of Ivory and Horn are mythological gates of Morpheus and Hypnos through which dreams pass. The Gate of Horn is the hallmark for true dreams; the Ivory Gate, said to be deception or false dreams (or falsely interpreted dreams, according to Synesius of Cyrene, schooled by Hypatia).

Chicory and Cornflower are sometimes confused. Both come from the family Asteracaea.

Copper Underwing: The Exeter Book, the largest known collection of Old English literature, is a 10th century codex of Anglo Saxon poems, many of which describe something and ask *What Am I?* Many of the ninety sum riddles contain double entendres.

The Mormo Maura is the Old Maid Moth native to Europe and has coloring similar to the moth I found in Oregon.

One legend of the Sphinx posits that she sat outside the city of Thebes and devoured men who couldn't answer her riddle.

A homunculus is a representation of little human sort of magical being. In some texts, a homunculus is created in sexual unions. In modern medical language, a homunculus, or an image of a miniature human-like body is said to live on the crown of the head, having first inhabited the soft part of the baby's skull. There is increasing evidence that this corticol homunculus, named by Wilder Penfield, controls somatosensory pain and pleasure in the physical body.

Slips, parapraxes, word plays and the neologism of dreams are psychoanalytic methods of uncovering riddles and complexes that lie in the subconscious. A neologism, in Psychiatry, refers to the use of words that have particular internal meanings to the person using them that may differ or vary from common usage. The psychoanalyst Jacques Lacan refers to these words and phrases as *signifiers*.

The Io moth is a brightly colored yellow (male) or coppery (female) moth found in the United States that displays prominent wing spots, similar to spots on the moth I saw.

Xanadu: The Stacie Cassarino epigraph is from her poem "New York Sonnets," *Zero at the Bone*, New Issues Poetry and Prose, Western Michigan University, 2009.

"In Xanadu... where Alph the sacred river ran... Weave the circle round him thrice... his flashing eyes, his floating hair," are lines from Coleridge's Kubla Khan.

Capriole is a *posse* leap for the horse. In it, the Lipizzan jumps, tucks his forelegs under and then extends his back legs in a kick in the air. The Lipizzans date back, in some sense, to the late first millenia when horses were brought from the Moors into Spain, but the Lipizzan breed specifically perfected "Airs above the ground " in the Spanish Riding School in Austria sponsored by the Hapsburg dynasty. The first stallion in the Lipizzan line was Pluto, foaled in 1765.

Hormones that stir a fetus: There is a hormone excreted from the baby's adrenal glands when it is really for labor to begin. The adrenal hormone secreted by the baby is picked up by the mother's pituitary gland, extending her womb, dilating her cervix, breaking her water and causing contractions to begin. The significance of this is that the baby itself determines the moment of birth and precipitates it by means of an interactive feedback system.

Ir Rahman, Ir Rahim is the pronunciated and sometimes favored spelling of the second and third phrases of the Quran in the Bismallah prayer. (*Al Rahman Al Rahim* are alphabetic transliterations.) In the prayer, these words are often translated as *most graceful* and *most merciful*. Linguistically, both words share the triliteral root (r-h-m), the first of which implies compassion for the believer and the unbeliever both, and the second of which is an attitude of ongoing compassion or tenderness. The root (r-h-m) has additional meanings of womb, kinship and relationship. Ancient Arabic, like most ancient languages, is a coded language (a gematria) in which letters are also numbers and make ciphers.

The Fibonacci sequence is a set of numbers in the sequence 0, 1, 1, 2, 3, 5, 8, 13... in which each number (after the initial 0 and 1) is the sum of its two previous numbers. As the numbers increase and are successively divided into their successors, they approach and get closer (and closer) to the golden ratio (1.6180339887...). Both the Fibonacci numbers and the golden ratio are blueprints for life forms. Pine cones, cauliflower, sunflowers and seedpods manifest in Fibonacci numbers and spiral from their centers in and out in proportion to the golden mean. The golden mean forms the spiral for Nautilus shells, rams' horns, the inner ear and spiral galaxies.

Slow twitch sinews are muscles that quiver when they are contracted. They are known for endurance.

Corboda, a city in Andalusia, was capital of the Caliphate during the height of the Arabic Empire. One author calls Cordoba the custodian of cultures during the Dark Ages. It is considered the gateway whereby the culture of Arabs and Moors entered the West.

Fouette (in ballet) is to turn with speed and grace in a way that whips around the body in a circle. The dancer's gaze remains fixed on a stable spot.

The Augean Stable in Greek mythology was a stable inhabited by immortal livestock. It had never been cleaned. One of the Twelve Labors of Heracles was an assignment to clean the stable. To do this, Heracles rerouted the underground river Alpheus. The reference in my poem is in removing the refuse and defecation of inaccurate projections and rumor. When we do this, and there is a mystic complex (or divine communion) at the center, *can we look on that without tearing it down?*

Charles Lamb, the English essayist and literary critic, was a life long friend of Coleridge.

Owls are of the order *Strigiforme*.

Higher Math: Rational numbers are what most people consider regular numbers and they include fractions. Algebraics include irrational numbers, e.g., the square root of 2 and the square root of 3. Transcendentals include numbers like Pi and *e*. Transfinite numbers (and patterns) run in an infinite sequence without end. The word *transfinite*, like the Cantor Set, was coined by Georg Cantor. Mathematical constants (numbers that appear over and over again, like Pi, Phi, etc.) are transfinite.

Eye of God: A ternary is a third, e.g., the middle third of the Cantor Set.

The sea shell, cochlea, etc. are examples of life forms that repeatedly spiral into manifestation in the mathematical form of Phi, also called the golden mean, or the golden ratio.

The Other, Ourselves: In Astrology, the moon's nodes, from the old Arabic and Chaldean systems, are *caput* and *cauda draconis,* visible on everyone's horoscope. Nodes refer to places the moon crosses the elliptic (the apparent path of the sun, viewed from earth, around the belt of the stars). The body of Draconis, the symbolic dragon (which I postulate as the karmic significator of the character, nature and path of the soul's larger struggle through many lifetimes) could theoretically be ascertained by imaging nodal points as they intersect and bounce through relationships with other signs, houses, rulerships, planets and nodes in the chart. Each planet, not only the moon, has nodes informing dimensions of the dragon's scales. The dragon cannot be directly glimpsed but only fathomed by witnessing patterns and repeating signatures (in the chart, life, memory, relationships, etc.) in fractal-like form. In order to grasp fractals in the experiential sense, we have to conceive of patterns and repeating signatures multi-dimensionally and multi-modally.

The vector of vision refers to the way nodes are points of subjective relativity, i.e., they don't objectively exist as distinct points in space. They exist relative to our subjective position on earth looking out across the zodiacal plane toward the stars. The significance of this, to me, is that we can only fathom the unfathomable by witnessing it at particular moments when it intersects subjective reality.

Photo by Mark Arinsberg
www.arinsberg.com

Julie Weber (born in Cleveland, Ohio) is author of two Poetry books: *The Cantor Set* and *Resin* (Love's Body), available on Amazon and through local libraries and booksellers. For more than a dozen years, Julie did counseling and Clinical Social Work in Ashland, Oregon. She was recipient of a *Lambda Literary Fellowship* in 2010 and was the winner of the 2011 *Dana Award* for Poetry.

Poems (from other work) appear or have appeared on *Oregon Poetic Voices* and in *Alligator Juniper, OCHO, Harrington Lesbian Fiction Quarterly, Dark Moon Lilith, We'Moon* and in the anthology *In the Spirit of We'Moon*. Julie has been a recent finalist/semi-finalist in the *Tupelo Snowbound, Oscar Wilde, Chroma, Orlando, Joy Harjo, Alligator Juniper and Lexi Rudnitsky* competitions.

(*The Cantor Set* was a finalist in the 2011 *Tupelo Snowbound*.)

www.ingramcontent.com/pod-product-compliance
Lightning Source LLC
Chambersburg PA
CBHW020024050426
42450CB00005B/627